Don't Let The Fear Win

How To Get Out Of Your Own Way
And Grow Your Business...Fast

Greg Faxon

To Emma

Who helped make this book a reality through her loving support, brilliant editing, and occasional kicks in the butt. You are my partner, teacher, and best friend. Thank you for everything you do.

DOWNLOAD THE AUDIOBOOK FOR FREE!

READ THIS FIRST

As a thank you for buying my book, I'd like to give you the Audiobook version completely free:

To download, go to:
gregfaxon.com/audiobook

Table of Contents

Warmup — 5

Period 1: The Opponent — 9
- Your Opponent Is Not Your Competitor — 10
- Your Opponent Is You — 12
- Your Opponent Is Driven By Fear — 14
- Your Opponent Covers Its Own Tracks — 15
- Your Opponent Is Not Procrastination — 17
- Your Opponent Wants You To Stay Busy — 19
- Your Opponent Thinks It Is Keeping You Safe — 21
- Your Opponent Is Keeping You From Your Potential — 23

Period 2: The Champion — 25
- Champions Aren't Fearless — 26
- Champions Do The Emotional Training — 28
- Champions "Act As If" — 30
- Champions Are Losers — 32
- Champions Don't Need Success To Feel Worthy — 34
- Champions Are Driven By Love — 36
- Champions Don't Choke — 38
- Champions Focus On The Process — 40

Period 3: The Controllables — 43
- How To Create Winning Rituals — 44
- How To Perform At Your Peak — 46
- How To Find A Champion Coach — 48
- How To Be Coachable — 50
- How To Build A World-Class Team — 52
- How To Create Work-Life Synergy — 54
- How To Craft A Compelling Vision — 56
- How To Sell More Of Your Thing — 58

Overtime — 61

WARMUP

It's Your Time

In a world where it's easier than ever to start a business, actually growing that business can be surprisingly hard. And finding sound advice on how to do it can be even harder. That's why I wrote this book.

As a business growth coach for high-achieving entrepreneurs, I've helped hundreds of people just like you improve their businesses and their lives. I've interviewed leaders like Seth Godin about the exact themes in this book. I've been recognized as a top athlete in two different sports -- wrestling and Spartan Racing -- and I consciously apply the lessons I've learned from those sports to my business.

Here's what I've discovered: the way most entrepreneurs go about improving their performance is completely backwards. One simple shift -- from battling external obstacles to focusing on the inner game -- can mean the difference between growing your business fast...or continuing to struggle.

This book gives you the concepts and tools you need to transform your mindset, your performance, and your business so that you can become a champion; someone who not only succeeds at what they do, but actively models the change that they want to see in the world.

If you take action on the concepts described in this book, your income will go up, you'll make a more meaningful impact with your work, and you'll be able to spend more quality time with your friends and family.

Notice that I said "if you take action." Without action, information can never become transformation. I've made this book as compact and streamlined as possible so you can understand the principles behind peak performance and then set up the structures to support it.

Many of the concepts in this book have been borrowed from my experience as a wrestler. And, just like in a wrestling match, this book is broken up into three "periods." In Period One, we'll be talking about the nature of your opponent (hint: it's not your competition). In Period Two, you'll learn the mindsets and attitudes of a champion entrepreneur. And in Period Three, we'll narrow in on the seven specific things you need to do in order to take your business to the next level.

All three periods are based around one critical concept, an equation developed by author Timothy Gallwey. That equation is:

$$Performance = Potential - Interference.$$

I believe that your potential, your capacity to contribute your gifts, is unlimited. But if your performance isn't where you want it to be, chances are there's something interfering with the natural realization of your potential. What exactly is interfering?

That's what we'll be talking about in Period One. Deep down, you already have everything you need to grow your business. It's just a matter of identifying what's stopping you, clarifying your vision, and then taking tangible steps towards building your ultimate business.

The ideas you're about to learn have created dramatic and long-lasting results for my clients. Each subsequent period will give you new insights as you strive to grow your business and become the champion entrepreneur you are meant to be.

It's time to get out of your own way and take control of your performance. Are you game?

PERIOD ONE
The Opponent

Your Opponent Is Not Your Competitor

Do you ever get stuck in "the loop"? The loop is when you're checking out different people's websites in your industry, scrolling endlessly down your social media feed, and then doing the whole thing all over again. As seductive as the loop can be, I'll bet you feel pretty drained after all that comparison.

Most entrepreneurs spend a lot of time looking at what their competitors are doing. They're driven by a zero-sum mentality, believing that every client or customer their competition gains is one that they've personally lost. And so they try to beat the competition at their own game, mimicking other people's styles and sacrificing their own.

This way of thinking has never produced a remarkable business. Ever. If you're playing by someone else's rules, the game is already over.

Your competitor isn't the problem. Neither is the hot new marketing hack that was supposed to make you six figures in one day. All of these things are part of the outer game of business.

It's easy to spend a lot of time and attention on the outer game. After all, it's the most obvious. The outer game includes the strategies, tactics, and techniques of business.

But there's another game being played at the same time: the inner game. These are the beliefs, mindsets, and emotional habits of the entrepreneur.

The vast majority of people spend about 90% of their time focused on the outer game and only about 10% of their time focused on the inner game.

Here's the problem with that approach...

At the highest levels of performance, in any domain, success is really 90% inner game and 10% outer game. The percentages are completely flipped. Yet most of the resources for growing your business focus on the areas which yield the least impressive and hardest to sustain results.

As you become more and more successful as an entrepreneur, your edge is going to come more and more from mastering the inner game.

In other words, it's not about your competitors at all. It's about you.

Your Opponent Is You

Before I was an entrepreneur, I was a wrestler.

As a freshman in highschool, I went 0-2 at the Prep National Wrestling Tournament.

If you had been in the stands before those two matches, you would have seen the surliest 103 pound kid in the world. All jacked up on Rocky movies and rap music. Nervous as hell.

Fast forward to senior year. Just before my All-American match, you'd see me sitting on the side of the mat with my eyes closed, listening to the sound of my breath. Meditating.

That match I became a Prep All-American.

What changed?

As a young athlete, I was good enough to qualify for Nationals. But not good enough to win there.

And while my technique improved as I became more experienced, the biggest difference wasn't what happened on the mat. It was what happened in my head.

The toughest opponent I ever faced was, well, me.

Only after accepting who my true opponent was could I get out of my own way. And once I learned how to win the inner game, the outer game largely took care of itself.

That's what this book is about. Because the transformation that a high-performing wrestler must go through to become a champion is the same transformation that you must go through if you want to become a champion entrepreneur.

This insight, that *you* are your biggest opponent, changes the game completely. It means that none of the outer games you've been playing are as important as the game you play on the inside.

The inner game of entrepreneurship probably isn't what you think it is. It isn't about giving yourself a pep talk or telling yourself to work harder. In fact, this book isn't about working harder at all. It's simply about exposing the lies that are slowing your business down.

Your Opponent Is Driven By Fear

The business of your dreams is within your reach. You have the technology. You have the ability to learn and make connections. You even have crowdfunding if you need to validate an idea.

The only remaining obstacle to growing your business is the one inside your own head: fear.

That's right. Fear is the only thing stopping you from fulfilling your potential as an entrepreneur.

This insight is both liberating and anxiety-provoking. Liberating because it means you already have everything you need to build a highly impactful business. Anxiety-provoking because it suggests that if you're not where you want to be, you have no one to blame but yourself.

Well, one part of yourself at least.

There are actually two parts inside all of us. There's the part driven by fear and the part driven by love. There's the scared little child who doesn't want to be rejected or forgotten about and the strong adult who's willing to give his or her gifts. From here on out, let's refer to these two parts as Little You and Big You.

So, how do you get rid of Little You and eliminate the fear once and for all?

You don't.

The real problem is not fear; it's your learned reaction to it. You've been conditioned to believe that fear is bad -- a sign that something is wrong -- and your default response when you feel it is to freeze or run away.

You will always have two selves. The goal is not to keep them separate. The goal is to have them wrestle together.

Your Opponent Covers Its Own Tracks

Are you starting to feel skeptical that your fear could be the only thing standing in the way of your business growth?

That's normal.

In fact, it's proof of how good your own mind is at shifting attention away from itself.

Out of all the tactics that your fear uses to elude you, the most insidious by far is a concept I call Creative Avoidance. If your opponent is fear, or what Steven Pressfield calls Resistance, then Creative Avoidance is one way that your fear manifests.

Creative Avoidance is the subconscious act of using one's imagination to prioritize peripheral tasks in order to avoid taking action on scarier, more important tasks.

Not only is Creative Avoidance invisible, but it covers its own tracks by creating the illusion that you're making progress. You convince yourself that what you are doing now is genuinely more important than the thing you should be doing.

And that's what makes Creative Avoidance more dangerous than any external conditions you'll face as an entrepreneur.

Ever get to the end of your day and wonder what you actually did? You're exhausted, and you know you were busy doing something, but you can't remember what? Simple: you Creatively Avoided.

It's not hard to remember doing the things that matter. The things that make us feel something. But Creative Avoidance is like alcohol: it numbs us, leaves us feeling mildly satisfied, and -- in the end -- keeps us stuck.

Fortunately, Creative Avoidance isn't perfect. Sometimes it leaves traces. The best way to overcome Creative Avoidance is by becoming aware of its patterns and then going head to head with it.

Your Opponent Is Not Procrastination

As a wrestler, I wasn't lazy. I didn't show up late for practice. I didn't drink or party with my friends. I didn't eat junk food one day and cut weight the next.

Like any good high-achiever, I got after it. I skipped the family meal on Thanksgiving so that I wouldn't be tempted (in retrospect this was a mistake - my mother wasn't very happy about it). I went running on Christmas morning because I knew my opponents would be taking the day off. I spent New Year's Eve doing heated yoga.

Unfortunately, my training quickly reached a point of diminishing returns. I was spending time working on my diet and fitness when I should have been wrestling against more challenging competition. At the end of the day, the most in-shape wrestler in the world will have trouble beating one who has spent more time on the mat against skilled opponents.

Why did I avoid competing with the best? Fear, of course. I was scared of failing.

I couldn't fail when I was killing myself at the gym. But I *could* give myself the illusion that I was doing everything I could to succeed. If you'd asked me whether I was prepared for Nationals, I would have said yes.

One day, my high school coach pointed out that none of the wrestlers in my local school league were pushing me anymore. I wasn't being challenged until the larger, end-of-season tournaments. And by then it was too late to learn from my mistakes.

From that point on, I focused my energy on practicing with and competing against people better than me. Since I was the best lightweight in my high school, I had to go outside of my practice room. I would look for the most highly ranked public school wrestlers in the state and show up at their practice. I even went to an application-only wrestling camp in an Ohio barn where we slept on the same mats we wrestled on. I got a pretty nasty skin infection from that one.

Once I started winning the inner game by facing my fear and wrestling against better competition, the outer game took care of itself. I started winning at the national level. It wasn't that I had been procrastinating, just that I was focused on the wrong things. The safe things.

It was only when I learned to recognize and confront my Creative Avoidance that I could reach my full potential as an athlete.

Whereas procrastination stems from laziness and is largely conscious, Creative Avoidance is rooted in fear and happens below the surface. Doing work that matters is scary and our minds are good at coming up with explanations for why we shouldn't get started quite yet (e.g. I just need to get a little stronger, do a bit more research, make my website better first).

Procrastination is what separates a novice from a high-achiever. But Creative Avoidance is what separates a high-achiever from a champion.

Your Opponent Wants You To Stay Busy

When you're Creatively Avoiding, you usually know it in your heart.

Problem is, we don't check in with our hearts much. We just try to stay in motion. Anything to avoid the fear and doubt inherent to entrepreneurship.

When you're busy, you don't have time to see what you're avoiding. It's only when you slow down that you're forced to confront the bold actions that would have the biggest impact on your business.

But bold actions are scary. That's why your fear of rejection works so hard to keep you occupied through Creative Avoidance.

Saying yes to things that don't align with your business goals? Creative Avoidance.

Collecting more tools and apps to get the work done instead of actually doing it? Creative Avoidance.

Gathering more information through books and courses than you really need in order to take that next step? Creative Avoidance.

As an entrepreneur, you shouldn't be proud of busyness. If you feel like you have too much on your plate, that's because you do.

Busyness is a symptom of unclear priorities. The busier we are, the harder it is to hone in on what really impacts our bottom line. This is why my counterintuitive prescription for most entrepreneurs who want to grow their business is to do *less*.

Your opponent wants to distract you. It comes at you fast, hoping that you will react instinctively and go in a thousand different directions. Don't play its game. Only by taking time to pause are you able to sidestep its advances.

We'll talk more about how to do that in Period 3. For now, understand that your priorities will become clear when you give yourself the space to see them.

Your Opponent Thinks It Is Keeping You Safe

You are evolutionarily wired to protect yourself from danger. But the fear that you feel as an entrepreneur isn't always rational. Most of the time you're reacting to a perceived risk, not an actual threat (when was the last time you got chased by a woolly mammoth?).

This misplaced fear comes from Little You, the one that doesn't want to disappoint anybody, be judged, or fail.

This is the part of you that freaks out when you leave your job to pursue a new business full-time, even though you know you're ready. It's the part of you that decides you went too far in that blog post, even though your vulnerability inspires everyone who reads it. And it's the part of you that doesn't ask for the sale, even though you know that your product or service is a perfect fit for that person.

The more closely aligned your work is with your passions, the scarier that work will be. Fear and desire go hand in hand. If the outcome didn't matter to you, you wouldn't feel the need to control it.

If you take a second now to think of something that scares you, you'll probably be able to feel where Little You lives. Is it in your stomach, your solar plexus, your chest? Wherever you feel the butterflies, that's Little You.

Little You thinks it is keeping you safe. But its logic is flawed. Little You's thinking is based on a world where you are small and helpless, before you learned how to take care of yourself.

That's where Big You comes in.

Think of Big You as the parent and Little You as the child. A parent's job is to help their child feel safe while providing the independence and confidence they need to grow. Big You needs to love, listen to, and take care of Little You *without* letting it call the shots.

If Big You doesn't step up, Little You will start to freak out. When that happens, all major growth comes to a halt.

Your Opponent Is Keeping You From Your Potential

Let's take a look at two things that make Little You really upset:

1. **Uncertainty**. With uncertainty comes the possibility of risk, and with risk comes the possibility of danger. Creative Avoidance thrives in the face of uncertainty. When things are certain, we don't Creatively Avoid, we just execute. Entrepreneurship is inherently uncertain; we make it up as we go along. Little You doesn't like this.

2. **Judgment**. If there is an opportunity to look stupid, be judged, or get rejected, Little You feels unsafe. It would rather not make too many waves. Again, this is in conflict with almost everything that an entrepreneur must do to succeed. Which is why Big You must never stop wrestling with Little You.

Little You doesn't want to feel scared. But if what you're doing doesn't scare you, it's probably not very valuable.

There are plenty of other entrepreneurs, and definitely plenty of employees, who are willing to learn more, work harder, and adhere to the status quo more closely than you are. These are attributes left over from the industrial economy, and they are not scarce. Since they're not scarce, they're not all that valuable.

What's scarce today is people who are willing to overcome their Creative Avoidance, be vulnerable, and become the best in the world at what they do.

As Seth Godin said in our interview together:

> "We don't do physical labor for a living anymore...most of us do emotional labor. And the question is, what is difficult about emotional labor?...The difficult task is confronting the fear of

> failure. That's what we are paid to do. That's what we are rewarded for."

In the information age, information was scarce. But now that information is abundant, it's not as valuable.

As Seth Godin points out, we've entered the connection economy. What's scarce now is people who are willing to put in the emotional labor necessary to connect with others.

And *because* that type of bravery is scarce, it's ultimately what you get paid most for. It's also what gives you more freedom and allows you to impact people on a deeper level. The only thing holding you back from having these things now is your ability to get out of your own way.

With practice, you can learn how to do that.

Intrigued? It's time for Period Two.

PERIOD TWO
The Champion

Champions Aren't Fearless

If you believe that bravery pays, it's easy to assume that feeling fear is a bad thing. But here's the truth: champions aren't fearless.

In fact, they expose themselves to *more* fear and discomfort than most people. The only difference is that champion entrepreneurs have a better relationship with their fear.

Remember, fear comes from Little You. And Little You isn't ever going away. Essentially, you have two options:

1. Make enemies with your fear and try to push it down.
2. Make friends with your fear and learn from it.

If you're like most entrepreneurs, you've chosen option one. You see fear as something to be "handled." When Little You gets scared, you try to ignore it.

If you've been using this strategy up until now, you may have realized that it doesn't work too well. That's not the relationship you would want with your child, and it's not the relationship you want with yourself.

Since you can't get rid of Little You, the best thing you can do is love it. Give it a name. When it cries, listen to it.

Listening to Little You does not mean doing everything it says. Often, you'll need to do the opposite. If you had a four-year-old child, you wouldn't let them plan your entire day. If you did, you'd both just end up on the couch eating Reese's. It's okay to acknowledge the part of you that wants to be comfortable without letting it dictate your business decisions.

Champion entrepreneurs know that their fear is a signpost, pointing them towards the most meaningful actions in their business. They've learned that the things they Creatively Avoid are also the things they are most passionate about. So they follow the fear.

It's easy to take yourself off the hook by assuming that this type of bravery is reserved only for the chosen few. But that mindset isn't likely to get you very far as an entrepreneur.

Champions Do The Emotional Training

Bravery is a muscle. It's something that you can strengthen over time. The best way to do this is to start with one keystone habit.

My first keystone habit was writing a weekly blog post. Writing scared the crap out of me, and having to do it every week put pressure on that bravery muscle, helping it grow.

Some people take cold showers every morning. Just knowing that it's going to be cold and having to step into the shower anyway helps create a new learned response to fear.

So, what makes you uncomfortable?

The best way to build the habit of bravery is to start small and go from there. If it paralyzes you, start smaller. Just like you can't lift a weight that exceeds your physical strength, you can't take an action that exceeds your current emotional strength.

Don't try to bench press 500 pounds right out of the gate. Either the bar won't move or you'll hurt yourself. Take a few plates off first.

If you're on a first date, and you're too scared to go in for the kiss, try holding her hand first.

If you want to leave your job, and it feels too high-stakes, build your business on the side first.

This same principle holds true every time you want to go bigger as an entrepreneur. If you want to go big, start small.

Before I wrote this book, I wrote a 16 page PDF about Creative Avoidance. It wasn't much, but it gave me the experience of producing something longer than a blog post. The positive feedback I got from it built the momentum and confidence that resulted in this book.

If your goal is to get stronger, trying to lift too much at once is just as useless as lifting too little. You'll know you've found the sweet spot when you're far enough outside of your comfort zone to feel butterflies, but not so far that you're paralyzed by fear.

Just know this: if you stay inside of your comfort zone for long enough, your bravery muscle will eventually atrophy.

Champions "Act As If"

If you've never lifted a certain amount of weight before, or wrestled against a certain caliber of opponent, or taken your business past a certain level, you have two options: give it a shot or plateau indefinitely. The only option if you want to grow is to act as if you have what it takes.

Muhammad Ali is often quoted as saying "I am the greatest, I said that even before I knew I was." Ali wasn't the most humble fighter, but he knew how to act as if he was already the boxer that he wanted to become.

And it worked. By doing what champions do, Muhammad Ali eventually became one.

You don't need to believe you are the best salesperson in the world in order to spend a lot of time selling. You don't need to believe you are the best writer in the world in order to write daily. You don't need to believe you are a high-end service provider in order to be more discerning about which clients you take on.

In the beginning, it really doesn't matter whether you *believe* you're a champion or not. If you want to become a champion, you must behave like one now.

Over time you'll see yourself taking consistent, meaningful action and you'll naturally start to think and feel like a champion. Social psychologist Daryl Bem calls this self-perception theory: we draw inferences about who we are by observing our own behavior first. In other words, our attitudes follow our actions, not the other way around.

Will acting like a champion guarantee that you will become the best in the world at something? Not necessarily. But if you don't act like a champion, I can guarantee you'll never be one.

Champion status isn't somewhere to get to, it's a place to come from. If you think that you'll start acting like a champion and giving your gifts *after* you've finally made it, you're fooling yourself. Be a champion now.

How would you act if you believed that you were already worthy? If you didn't need any justification or validation for doing what you wanted to do?

Well, you'd probably start doing things with the only justification being "because I get to." You'd increase your prices, close more sales, and be more bold in your marketing communications.

Ask yourself:

What would Richard Branson do in this situation? Or Jay-Z? Or Oprah? Choose someone you respect to model your decisions after and you will start to become a champion in your own right.

Most entrepreneurs wait for clarity before taking action. They get stuck looking for a sign that success is certain. Champion entrepreneurs know that taking action is the best answer to almost any question they have - including whether or not they have what it takes to be the best at what they do.

Here's the funny thing: when you finally start acting like a champion, you'll probably end up as a loser. At least for a little while...

Champions Are Losers

Acting like a champion means going up against the big guys. It means taking bold action. It means putting yourself out there in ways you never have before. And when you do those things for the first time, it's likely that you'll fail.

When I started to wrestle against better competition, I started losing a lot more. Sometimes this made me embarrassed. Mostly, it made me better.

In business, losing often appears in the form of a "no." Most people don't like hearing this word. But guess what?

If people don't have the opportunity to say "no" to what you offer them, they also don't have the opportunity to say "yes." Which means that the amount of times you'll hear the word "yes" will be directly proportional to the amount of times you hear the word "no."

This point is worth underscoring: champion entrepreneurs are successful because they've heard *more* "no's" than you, not less.

For this reason, you shouldn't be proud of a perfect record. A perfect record means that you didn't put yourself out there often enough to make small failures.

Seth Godin puts it nicely in his book *Poke The Box* when he says, "If I fail more than you, I win." You don't want to fail so big that you get knocked out of the game forever, but you do want to fail more than your opponents.

You may think that you can avoid failure by playing small and never getting rejected. But if you haven't tried, you are already in a state of failure. You've said "no" to yourself before anyone else has had the opportunity to say "yes." There's a 100% guaranteed chance of failure at this point.

High-performers don't like to fail. It's hard and scary and embarrassing. So when most people finally reach a comfortable level of success, they cling on to it for dear life. They stop taking risks that might jeopardize their hard-earned sense of security.

And they stagnate.

Champions know that the only way you get really good at anything is by failing at it first. They accept short-term failure as the price of long-term success. They don't let the fear of a bruised ego keep them from achieving continually greater things.

Perfection isn't the goal of a champion. Success is. And success requires failure.

Champions Don't Need Success To Feel Worthy

The only way to truly embrace failure is by separating your results in business from your worth as a human being.

Unfortunately, most high-performers believe that their worthiness comes from what they achieve. They've been taught from an early age that they will become more valuable as humans if they make more money or have more of an impact.

Champions don't use success or failure as a way of defining who they are. They know that they can be a champion in the midst of failure, just as they can be a novice in the midst of success.

Here's the truth: what you do is not the same as who you are. Your worth as a human does not fluctuate moment to moment, even if your perception of yourself does.

Have you ever had a moment of feeling complete exactly as you were? This is proof that your outside circumstances don't need to dictate how worthy you feel.

If you choose to define yourself through your results, be ready to ride an emotional roller-coaster on a daily basis. If you view every business misstep as evidence of your inherent unworthiness, rather than a natural part of the entrepreneurial process, you'll always be reliant on external validation.

And you'll get stuck. Because you'll be waiting for permission to take action instead of assuming you have what it takes to be successful. Worthiness needs to come before success, not after.

On the occasions when you *do* have success in your business, the feeling of achievement will be fleeting. Why? Because you'll find something new to chase in order to feel whole.

Worthiness is not an additive process. It's a subtractive one. Everything you need is already inside of you. It's just a matter of peeling away your outer protective layers in order to expose it.

When you finally accept that nothing is wrong with you, you stop looking outside yourself for other people's strategies and hacks. You start to discover your own way of doing things. And you start focusing on the inner game a lot more.

Champions Are Driven By Love

At any given moment, there is a game being played between Big You and Little You. The quality of that relationship is going to have a huge impact on your performance. And, as with any relationship, the best ones are grounded in love.

When I was a young wrestler, I trained and wrestled *not* to lose. Then I wrestled to win, which was an improvement. But both of those goals were ultimately driven by fear. When I wrestled to win, I was still a victim of outside circumstances.

Most high-performers are the same way. They feel compelled to perform only in order to prove themselves, or to avoid disappointing others. They focus on moving away from what they don't want instead of moving *towards* the things they do want.

By default, we are wired to be more motivated by the idea of what we could lose than of what we could gain. So it's natural that we continue trying to get leverage on ourselves that way.

But if you want to transform your business into something remarkable, you have to stop using fear and scarcity as your primary motivation.

Champion entrepreneurs are driven by love. They love the work that they do, they love helping the people that they're meant to serve, and they love mastering their craft. As an athlete, my best performances came when I was wrestling for the love of the game. I've found the same to be true with my clients.

Creativity cannot flourish in the face of fear. When Little You hijacks the system, entrepreneurship becomes about finding and following the right formulas. Fueled by Little You's paranoia, we accumulate more and more information instead of trusting that we have the answers already.

Is it possible to achieve short-term success by using fear as your primary motivator? Of course. But why would you want to?

Little You reacts much better in the long term to love than it does to fear. So don't beat yourself up when you're not performing at your full capacity. Don't

try to push Little You down. Instead, be grateful for that part of you and acknowledge all the awesome things you've already done.

In dating, people often talk about learning to love yourself first. It's not all that different in business. If you can't be your own biggest fan or your own most loyal client, how can you expect anyone else to follow suit?

Most entrepreneurs try to use anxiety as a strategy. They try to improve themselves through criticism and comparison. But as Martin Luther King Jr. said, "Darkness cannot drive out darkness; only light can do that."

The paradox of performance is that only by accepting yourself exactly as you are do you create the space necessary for change.

Champions Don't Choke

When you are driven by fear, you tend to become overly attached to a narrow range of acceptable results. That's because you think that the success of your business determines the success of your life. But by holding on so tightly to a specific outcome, you actually end up performing worse.

Champions don't fall into this trap. They live by the mantra "High Intention, Low Attachment."

The champion entrepreneur has high intention: a strong desire to create a certain type of change in the world.

But champions also have low attachment to that change happening in a certain way (or even happening at all). That's because they are already whole. They don't need a specific result to happen in order to feel complete.

Have you ever been on a date with someone who had high intention, high attachment? I'll bet they came off as desperate and controlling.

It's essential to have a strong desire to create something for the people you serve, but your attachment to that result is counterproductive.

We only choke when we overthink things, and we only overthink things when we are overly attached to the outcome.

When you grasp at success, when you view succeeding as something you *have* to do, as opposed to something that you want to do, you become needy. And when you do that, you repel the very clients, customers, and fans you hope to attract.

Having a high attachment mindset gives you tunnel vision. It doesn't leave you open to new opportunities and ways of doing things. A low attachment mindset is critical if you want to be able to change and adapt in the moment.

What might happen if you took all of the energy you spend clinging to outcomes you can't control and used that energy to manage the process instead?

Champions Focus On The Process

Sometimes when I talk about detaching from the outcome, people hear it as "you should settle for mediocre results." But that's not what I'm saying. All I'm suggesting is that you shift your focus to something more productive.

When I was a young athlete, I wanted to win. But I couldn't control winning. I could only control the process: how hard I worked, how much fun I had, how present I was.

When I focused on the process, here's what happened: I felt less pressure, I worked harder, and I wrestled better. Oh yeah, and I started winning a lot more.

As an entrepreneur, the outcome of a specific sale isn't up to you. Whether or not your content goes viral isn't up to you. The only thing that matters is the process.

You might not be able to directly control how many people buy what you are selling, but you can control how many times you ask. You may not be able to control which pieces of content go viral, but you can control how many you produce.

Focusing on the process also makes you more confident because you quickly see that when you change the way you behave, it changes the outcomes you get.

You should celebrate a successful process just as much as a successful outcome. Sometimes that means celebrating failures, as failure is an important part of any good process. So if you high-five your wife every time you make a big sale, be sure you also high-five her after you put yourself out there and hear a "no."

I have a wrestling friend, let's call him Dave, who lost 5-6 in the quarter-finals of the state championships to someone he was clearly better than. How does Dave know he was better? Because he actually scored more points than the other guy.

What happened was that the ref awarded one of his takedowns to the other wrestler by accident and refused to adjust the points once the match was over. Basically, Dave got robbed.

Not a day goes by when Dave doesn't think about that match. Ask him about it and he'll tell you, "It's one of the best things that ever happened, because it taught me to never let anything in my life be that close again."

It's tempting as an entrepreneur to say the equivalent of "the ref screwed me" when people don't see your brilliance. In business, "the ref" is anything you can't directly control: potential clients, market conditions, the amount of hours in a day, etc. And it can be tempting to blame these external factors when things don't go the way you planned.

But as soon as you begin to blame the ref, you lose the inner game. Because you can't control what the market wants, or how many hours are in a day. The only thing you can control is aligning your product or service with a market need and clearly conveying its value.

If you do your job right, no small lapse in judgment will affect the success of your business. It will be obvious to the people you serve that your product or service is a great fit.

So you have a choice: make excuses or take responsibility for your process. As a champion entrepreneur, your job is to control the controllables.

PERIOD THREE
The Controllables

How To Create Winning Rituals

Every elite athlete has a pre-game ritual. A way to connect with their mission, visualize a successful outcome, and warm up their body and mind. This is the ultimate controllable in a sea of uncertainty.

You too can create daily, weekly, and even yearly rituals to help ground you, giving you a greater sense of control.

Out of all these rituals, your morning ritual is by far the most important. A champion knows that they have to start each day off strong. A winning morning ritual will accomplish this by addressing the three foundational areas required for peak performance:

1. **Emotional** - How can you set a strong foundation for your spirit? My morning starts with a 20-30 minute meditation and breakfast with my partner.
2. **Intellectual** - How can you set a strong foundation for your mind? My morning ritual includes reading and writing.
3. **Physical** - How can you set a strong foundation for your body? My morning ritual ends with a short bodyweight workout that always gives my energy a boost.

You might also consider having a weekly ritual. Not every day is a game day. I take Saturdays and Sundays as off days, Mondays and Fridays as training days (marketing and team coordination), and Tuesday through Thursday as game days (this is when I do my coaching).

You can build a similar flow into your year, having some months where you need to perform at your peak, others where you train, and still others that you take off.

These rituals will not only give you a sense of rhythm and stability, they'll also allow you to operate at your full capacity when the stakes are highest. Champion entrepreneurs accept the fact that no one can be "on" all the time. Then they structure their work and life accordingly.

One of the most overlooked functions of a ritual is simply to create space. In wrestling, there is a short break between periods for you to collect yourself and look to your coach. In business you need the same thing.

Champion entrepreneurs leave just enough space in their lives to check in and ask, "What is the next scary action I need to take?" Creative Avoidance, because it operates through busyness, doesn't want you to ask this question. It doesn't want you to tap into your intuition.

You must set up structures in your life that allow you to have that space. Maybe it's taking a full day off each week, not thinking about work at all. Maybe it's walking your dog in the middle of the day. Maybe it's a regularly scheduled call with your coach.

The key to productivity isn't doing more. It's doing less. You can't discover new ideas or solutions if there's no space for them to come in.

So when you're not sure how to spend your day, try doing nothing for a moment. Doing nothing is worse than doing the thing that matters, but it's much better than staying busy with useless tasks.

If you do nothing for long enough, you'll eventually create the space you need to see and do what really matters.

Of course, this can provoke a lot of anxiety for driven entrepreneurs who feel like they need to be doing things all the time. Let's talk about how to deal with that anxiety.

How To Perform At Your Peak

In athletics, the most nerve-racking part of a performance isn't the game itself. It's the twenty minutes before you start. Once the whistle blows, your fear turns into flow.

Flow is what happens when you are completely engaged in an activity, when your level of skill matches the challenge in front of you, when you lose track of time.

Most entrepreneurs spend the majority of their day inside of their heads and outside of the flow state. Champions make sure to stay in flow for as long as possible.

If you want to be more brave in business, you need to minimize the amount of time you spend in anticipation. Anticipation is the hardest part.

There are two ways to accomplish this: either try not to think about things you'll have to do in the future, or take action on them so fast that you have no time to think.

The first strategy is about presence. The best way to control your degree of presence is by noticing what is happening right now in this moment. Reading the words on this page. Listening to the sounds around you.

I encourage all of my clients to incorporate some sort of mindfulness practice into their work. This could mean doing a daily meditation, as we discussed in the last section, or it could mean simply focusing on your body and breathing before an important call.

When you're really present, you'll notice that some days you might not have the energy to work on your business. Maybe that's okay. What would happen if all you did was stay present, capitalizing on the times where your creativity was flowing and taking the rest of the time off?

I'm not advocating for laziness. In fact, I don't worry about laziness with my high-achieving clients. Most of them are so far towards the burn-out side of the spectrum that the best thing they could do is take time to recover instead of turning to Creative Avoidance.

The second thing that helps facilitate a flow state is momentum. You get momentum from taking small and consistent steps on something. The best way to do this is to stop planning and only focus on your next most important step.

Planning often interferes with doing. We can't execute at a high level while also thinking about what needs to get done in the future. Overthinking may feel like a protective mechanism, but it's not a very good one.

The key here is recognizing when it's time to plan versus when it's time to execute, and not attempting to blend the two.

When you combine presence and momentum, you naturally perform at your peak. Instead of watching from the side of the mat, you'll be in on the action. The next component you need is someone in your corner to help you adjust when something isn't working.

How To Find A Champion Coach

No Olympic champion has ever won gold without a fantastic coach. Why should business be any different? The truth is, no one makes it to an elite level of performance alone.

Coaches are different than mentors. Your coach doesn't need to be a better performer than you in your specific domain. But they do need to be an expert in facilitating your development.

Michael Phelps's coach, Bob Bowman, isn't a better swimmer than Michael Phelps. Michael Phelps is the best swimmer in the world. But Bowman can *see* Phelps better than any other person in the world.

He can see Phelps's potential. He can see where Phelps is holding back. He can clarify and hold Phelp's vision with him when it falters. That's the true value of a coach.

Entrepreneurs are just like athletes in this respect. My clients are too close to their own businesses to see their blind spots. I help them see exactly what is affecting their performance, create a strategy with them to overcome it, and then support them in taking action.

Some coaches get fooled by their client's Creative Avoidance. But champion coaches don't buy into the stories that their clients create. If you don't have a coach who can see where you're holding back, or doesn't call you out on it, go find one that can.

There are three main barriers to finding a champion coach:

1. **Comfort.** Maybe you already have a coach that you've been with for a while, and you feel like you're checking the box on it without being pushed too hard. Or maybe you don't have a coach yet, and you know that hiring one would require you to step your game up to a new level.

Remember: all significant growth happens outside of your comfort zone.

2. **Ego.** Some people resist getting a coach because they believe that they can get to the top on their own. Problem is, that's never happened in the history of elite performance. Successful entrepreneurs are proud of having a coach because they realize that it's one of the marks of being a champion.

3. **Knowing where to look.** There's a lot of smoke and mirrors in the coaching industry, and it can be hard to find someone you trust. At the end of the day, the most important things to consider when you're looking for a coach are referrals, results, and fit. Go with someone you know, who has a proven track record, and who you click with.

How To Be Coachable

It's not enough just to have a champion coach. You also have to be coachable.

Champion coaches can be multipliers for your business. As the client, you are one half of that equation. The more you put into your relationship with a coach, the more you'll get out of it.

Here are three components that will allow you to get exponential results from coaching. I've put them into the acronym A.C.T., which stands for:

A - Action: If you don't take action on the insights you get with your coach, your business won't grow. It's really that simple. Champion clients take full responsibility for their own results because they know that their coach isn't here to save them, validate their situation, or do the work in their place.

C - Courage: Are you willing to challenge yourself? If you are more committed to playing it safe than you are to growing your business, there's not much a coach can do for you. Your results will be directly proportional to the level at which you are willing to feel uncomfortable.

T - Trust: If you are constantly second-guessing your coach, or yourself, you'll always be going two steps forward and one step back. Part of what makes the coaching relationship so powerful is your belief that it's powerful. Your faith, openness, and willingness to learn are essential.

Bottom line: it isn't just about showing up on time. It's about taking the time to show up fully.

As an aside, it's worth realizing that your coach is human. The more that they feel appreciated, the more they'll put into the relationship. And saying thank you is only one part of gratitude.

You can also demonstrate your gratitude by making a bigger social impact through your work, sending your coach referrals, or passing along the lessons you learned from them.

How To Build A World-Class Team

Champion coaches are one component of your world-class team. Before we talk about how to build the rest of it, let's expand our definition of team.

Having a team doesn't necessarily mean having employees. You might have just a few select contractors or assistants to help you with projects. Your team might include colleagues or referral partners.

Basically, anyone who has influence over your business outcomes is a part of your team. If you don't acknowledge this, you won't give these people the energy and attention that they deserve.

Every entrepreneur already has a team. The question is: do you have a world-class team?

Teams become world-class when…

1. **Every individual member is operating in his or her core brilliance zone.** This includes you. It can be hard to let go of tasks if you feel you aren't worthy of doing just the things you love and are good at, or if you feel like you need to have control over everything. But the truth is, there are probably a lot of activities you do now that you shouldn't be doing. Find someone who can do them better, faster, or cheaper than you.

2. **The team is moving towards a shared vision using clear agreements and communication.** It's your job as a leader to make sure that your team knows the what, why, and how of the thing you are doing. If you notice that there are unmet expectations or resentment, it's your job to open up the lines of communication and create a new agreement.

3. **The whole is always greater than the sum of the parts (1+1=3).** In any relationship, the ultimate goal is to create a synergy that goes beyond just the collective output of each individual. If you've implemented the first two steps, and it still doesn't feel like you've achieved this, ask yourself what it would take in order to have the whole be greater than the sum of the parts. And if your team started out equaling three and now doesn't, it's a sign that something needs to change.

You are only as strong as the weakest link on your team. Yet oftentimes, just as with hiring a coach, our ego prevents us from getting the support that we need to grow, or from letting go of bad hires. Don't let that happen to you.

Your family and friends are also part of your team. Without their support it's going to be difficult to go the distance. Which brings us to our next insight…

How To Create Work-Life Synergy

If you think that you can have poor health or relationships and still perform at your peak in business, you're fooling yourself. You need to recognize that your performance in other areas of life impacts your performance in business just as much as your business impacts your life.

By investing in your health and relationships, you become a happier entrepreneur. Happy entrepreneurs create more value, build better businesses, and last longer than surly ones.

Problem is, you only have a limited amount of time and energy to distribute among each area of your life. That's why, if you want to be the best in the world at what you do, you need to say goodbye right now to the idea of work-life balance.

Trying to completely separate your life from your business means you're constantly going to be short-changing one or the other.

That's why champion entrepreneurs don't strive for work-life balance. Champions refuse to settle for less than the best in all areas of their life, and they know that the only way to accomplish this is through work-life synergy.

Your experiences as a parent or partner can help you overcome challenges at work. Lessons you've learned at work can be applied to your health and fitness. These areas do not need to take from each other - they can all contribute to a greater collective meaning.

The lines between my own work and life are so blurred that it can be hard to tell the difference. For example, my partner is helping edit this book. We live on an 80 acre property where we also host events and coaching intensives. While we both have our own businesses, they've evolved together and so they are constantly informing each other.

Keeping your work separate from your life can sometimes feel safer. It can feel like you're diversifying your risk. But the truth is, you can never truly separate the two spheres.

Work and life are always going to affect each other. So instead of trying to balance them, what if you acknowledged that and started being more intentional about how they were related?

The key here is to make sure that each area of your life serves multiple purposes, and that all of them are aligned with your greater values and sense of purpose.

Ask yourself: what components of my life am I keeping separate out of fear? How might I be able to create more synergy by integrating them?

How To Craft A Compelling Vision

As a wrestler, my vision was simple: I wanted to be on the prep All-American podium at the end of my senior year. When my training got intense, when I didn't feel like cutting weight any more, when I started to question why I was doing any of it in the first place, I could always picture getting handed my medal.

As a leader, you must have a clear vision of what success looks like as well. You can't know where you're headed or how to get there without one.

Compelling visions are usually very specific. You can't be the best in the world at everything, so choose the change you're most committed to and then optimize for it. Champions know that mastery requires focus, and they narrow their vision relentlessly.

This can be painful. If you're a high-performer, you could probably be successful at lots of different things. But only by choosing one or two will you be able to make a deep and lasting impact. You don't want to come to the end of your life having collected a bunch of gold medals for games you never wanted to play in the first place.

A truly compelling vision extends beyond just yourself. Unlike my vision as a wrestler, your vision should center primarily around the change that you most want to make for the people you serve. This is your Why.

A strong Why isn't just more motivating for you - it also inspires people who share your vision to get on board.

The Why of using good design to challenge the status quo is one of the big reasons Apple has been so successful. Steve Jobs had a vision of building "a computer for the rest of us", and he held onto it so strongly that what started in his imagination quickly became real. His ability to sell this compelling vision, both to himself and to others, is what enabled his team to create innovative products on incredibly tight deadlines and then market them successfully.

Simon Sinek, author of *Start With Why*, imagines a world where people wake up inspired to go to work. Tim Ferriss has a vision of creating world-class learners. Martin Luther King Jr. had a dream that his four children would live in a nation where they would be judged not by the color of their skin, but by the content of their character.

So, what's your version of winning the gold medal? What exactly does it look like? Most people confuse a vision with a mission statement, but what makes a vision so powerful is that you can actually picture it in your mind's eye.

Once you've crafted your vision, it's time to choose the trackable metric that will get you from where you are to where you want to go. Otherwise you'll have a great big vision and no concrete action steps to get you there.

For example, most writers track the number of pages they read and write each day.

For entrepreneurs, the most important metric is usually sales.

How To Sell More Of Your Thing

If you want to sell more of what you offer, spend more time selling.

When it comes to growing your business fast, this is the number one factor that is most within your control. Your vision can't become reality if nothing gets sold.

While there are many ways to become better at selling -- primarily by working on your inner game as described in Period 2 -- the biggest thing you can do to improve right now is simply to spend more time selling.

Not only does every additional hour of time spent selling increase your chances of growing your business in the short term - it also makes you better at sales in the long term.

Selling is the number one thing that most entrepreneurs Creatively Avoid. They will produce hours of content, work on their website, and learn more than anyone else about their area of expertise before they invite someone to a sales conversation.

If there's one thing that you take away from this book, I hope it's this: if you want to grow your business faster, you need to spend your time doing things that help you sell more.

Selling is one of the biggest triggers for Little You because it's impossible to avoid rejection. At some point, you're going to have someone say "no." It's much easier to just sit back and wait for your phone to ring.

Unfortunately, that's how you end up with no money and very little impact.

Most people Creatively Avoid selling because it feels pushy. But if you don't like selling, you're probably doing it wrong. Here are two ways to make the sales process more fun:

1. **Reframe selling.** From something manipulative to something transformative. Selling is one of the most important services that you provide for your customers and clients. If you don't help them make the decision to invest in what you are offering, or if they don't know what you have to offer them in the first place, they will never experience the benefit of it.

2. **Find your own way of selling.** One that feels authentic to you. Everyone has their own unique style, and the way I sell will look different from the way you sell. Anything that feels icky can be done in a different and better way. When you view selling as an extension of the product or service you offer, you put more intention into the sale.

How do you learn *your way*? You guessed it. You spend more time selling.

By writing down how many minutes you spend in sales calls each day, you won't be able to hide from it. And if you have a team that does the selling for you, then track how much time they spend on sales calls. This one metric creates a cascading effect of productive behaviors for you as an entrepreneur.

If you want to increase the time you spend selling, you'll also have to find new ways to bring in leads. So you'll quickly identify and execute the marketing activities that are highest leverage.

Selling is at the center of every business. When you focus on it, you naturally do the activities on the periphery that support it. And, as long as you're selling the right thing to the right people, you're moving your vision forward.

So, what are you going to do today to sell more of your thing?

It's time to get out of your own way and grow your business fast.

OVERTIME

More Than A Game

As a champion, your work is never done. If you continue to push your edge, you'll continue experiencing fear and Creative Avoidance. In other words, the match goes on forever.

And that's okay. Because I believe that entrepreneurship is not just about building a profitable business. Entrepreneurship is a channel through which you can actualize your fullest potential.

This doesn't mean staking your worth as a human on what you achieve at work. It means taking advantage of every opportunity to learn and grow. Achievement is simply one byproduct of this.

When you view business as a chance to realize your potential, it changes how you play the game. You don't have to get frustrated anymore when challenges come up. Obstacles are just one more chance to become the champion you were meant to be.

In wrestling, the person who wins in overtime isn't necessarily the strongest or most skilled athlete. It's the person who goes the distance. The one who has so much passion for the game itself that they are more focused on following through than on winning.

The root of the word passion is *passio*, which in Latin means to suffer. To endure. It's the entrepreneur who is most willing to suffer for their business who will build something that lasts.

For me, giving my gifts isn't just about making more money. It's bigger than that.

I have a friend named Zack who lost his speech and short-term memory after being hit during a high school football game. I remember visiting him at the hospital and seeing a dent in the side of his head where the doctors had removed a piece of his skull. It shook me to my core.

Watching someone who had so much potential be robbed of his gifts in a single moment changed the way I viewed the world. Chances are, you've had a moment yourself where you've realized how precious life is. This should change the way you view your business.

If, like me, you believe that entrepreneurship is a channel through which to actualize your full potential, then you are morally obligated to give your gift. You're obligated because there are people like Zack who don't have the ability to give their gift in the same way anymore.

The only question is, what are you going to do about it?

As you think of your answer, remember the thesis of this book: if it doesn't scare you, it's probably not worth doing at all.

Because if the thing you're doing today doesn't scare you even a little bit, you're not growing your business -- or your own potential -- as fast as you could be.

Whether it's building a team, hiring a great coach, selling more, marketing yourself in a new way, or changing the entire course of your business, the thing that scares you most is exactly what you should be doing right now.

Let the inner games begin.

Thank You

The reason I wrote this book was to help unleash the potential of people who seek to make a positive impact on the world. Basically, people like you.

If you've made it this far, I hope you'll go to **gregfaxon.com/contact** and shoot me an email introducing yourself. Tell me what you're working on. Tell me where you're feeling challenged. I'd love to see how I can support you.

Acknowledgments

Don't Let The Fear Win has made me acutely aware of the people I have in my corner who make doing this work possible. I'll try my best to list the ones that come to mind most readily, but I know that some very important people will inevitably be left out. Please know that your support has not gone unnoticed.

I'll start with Emma, to whom I have dedicated this book. She turned what started off as a jumbled mess into what you're reading now. She is a champion.

The second dedication I would have added, if people did that sort of thing, would have been to my family. To my mom and dad, who modeled and encouraged bravery every single day of my childhood. My mom for making it out of that small town with low expectations and into her own business. My dad for beating a potentially fatal spinal tumor and then treating it like a gift. And to Hilary, who has always gone out of her way to be the best big sis in the world, including during the final round of edits for this book. I love you all very much.

I also want to thank some of the fantastic coaches and mentors that I've been fortunate enough to learn from. Christina Berkley for being the number one catalyst of my coaching business and, more importantly, for helping me reconnect with Little Greg. Seth Godin for showing me what it means to be a leader. Plus Jonathan Fields, Kyle Cease, Eben Pagan, and many more virtual mentors for inspiring me and teaching me.

Thank you to Timothy Galloway for pioneering the concept of the inner game. To Jan Black for helping me see and articulate my core brilliance. To Adam Holland and Mike Marshall for showing me what truly powerful coaching is all about. To Mollie Coons for working her design magic on the book. To Smiley Poswolsky for providing fantastic advice during the writing and marketing process. To Clif Cody for managing my launch like a champ. To Geoff Welch, Nick Snapp, and others for reading early versions of the book and providing feedback. To my team of loyal fans who agreed to read, review, and evangelize the book: Guerric, Matthew, Geoff, Joseph, McKenna, Kyle, Clarence, Oren, and Jack.

Finally, I want to thank all of my other incredible clients and readers who make the work I do possible. I don't take your attention for granted.

Made in the USA
San Bernardino, CA
08 September 2016